LIFE

HAIKU
BY
HAIKU

a book of poetry
by jan morrill

Printed in the United States of America

Book design and cover art by Andrea L. M. Hansen

BIRDSONG

Published by Birdsong Publishing, Dallas, Texas

ISBN-13: 978-0615957470
ISBN-10: 0615957471

This book of tiny poems is dedicated to the tiny soul in my life—my first grandchild, Tommy.

My little grandson

is here, the twinkle of the

twinkle in my eye

A WORD FROM THE AUTHOR

Why do I consider haiku one of the most powerful forms of poetry? Because it can express an entire story in only seventeen syllables. I've enjoyed writing this form for many years and even included several as introductions to many of the chapters in my historical fiction, *The Red Kimono*. (University of Arkansas Press, February 2013)

As with life, I believe the power of haiku is in its brevity. Many of my best memories have been the result of short, powerful moments in my life. I've tried to capture some of these moments in the haiku, senryu and tanka I've included in this book.

桜

first cherry blossoms
a petal almost touches
her red kimono

—JOHN HAN

WINNER OF OGHMA CREATIVE MEDIA

HAIKU CONTEST

NATURE

花

the first crocus pokes
bright yellow through icy snow
long winter's farewell

波

waves moving, growing
excitement building, rushing
calm, peaceful water

苺

tiny white petals
surround the first whisper of
anticipation
'til strawberries ripen and
sweetness bursts on my tongue

日

the birth of a day
sun rises out of darkness
a new beginning

冬

crisp air nips my nose
snowflakes dust my lashes
a walk in winter

秋

in the mist of fall
a red leaf spins to the ground
alone on the path

雨

splashing in puddles
how the rain washes away
my inhibitions

夏

sultry summer day
sunlight ripples through the leaves
buzz of cicadas

snowflakes waltz in wind
hushing nature with a touch
winter's white blanket

蝶

caterpillar weaves
its cocoon and a lovely
butterfly grows then
flits in the breeze, unaware
its end will come one day soon

竜

rabbit passed in
cold winter, but do not fear
dragon has arrived

星

twinkling stars travel
from distant galaxies to
grant an earthling's wish

春

yellow daffodils
dance in Spring breezes like the
giggles of nature

花

thorny and lifeless
but for shudders in the wind
then a flower blooms

鳥

at morning's first light
robin's sweet serenade is
nature's alarm clock

秋

when Autumn arrives
savor each color and know
winter will come soon

冬

Winter blows her cold
breath across my window while
crystals sparkle on
a soft, white carpet rolled out
to announce her arrival

long and rocky, with
twists and turns, until at last
a fork in the road

蝶

so many gardens
to find if the butterfly
would open its eyes

midnight crickets chirp,
yield to bird songs in pink light
symphony at dawn

damsel fly dances
skips along the water's edge
flirting with demise

水

clear water trickles
so long taken for granted
until it is gone

tiny, white snowflakes
dance in the darkness of night
while I drift to sleep

天

barren branches reach
in winter for the heavens
praying for rebirth

風

blow dandelions
and watch a thousand wishes
scatter in the wind

dogwood flowers bloom
delicate lace scattered like
whispers of spring

Spider on the wall
It stares. I glare. Showdown.
Who makes the first move?

蛙

the frog leaps forward
his mind focused only on
landing where he's aimed

日

a lovely flower
will wither and die without
a little sunshine

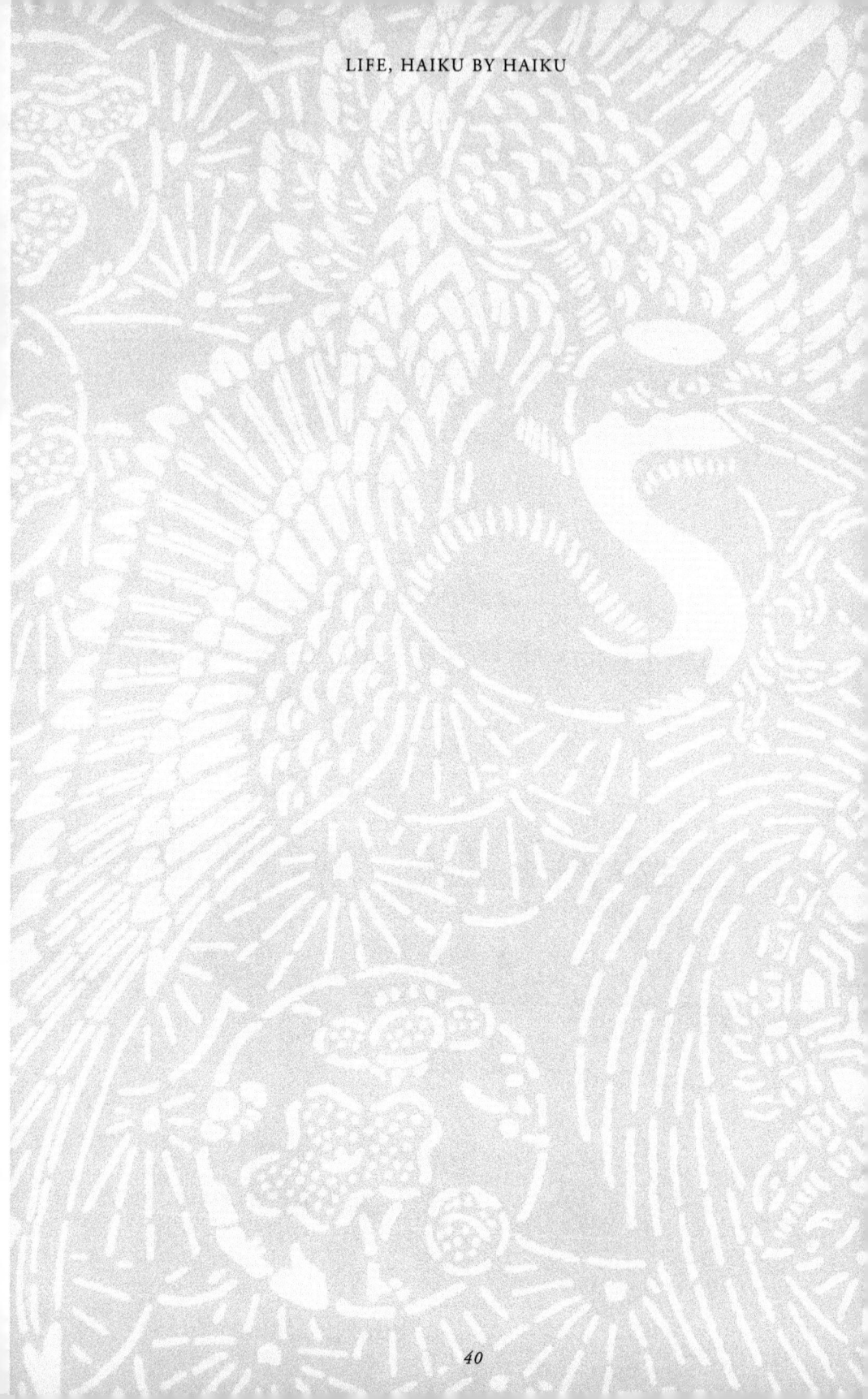

LOVE
&
LIFE

心

my heart locked away
until your heart knocked and asked
can she come to play?

if uncertainty
approaches in days ahead
look into my eyes

this tear on my cheek
once long-hidden, now a gift
trusted to your care

波

heartfelt words like waves
rush to your far away shore
lost in dark, vast seas

our bed is empty
train whistles in the distance
I hug my pillow

passion in our eyes
our bodies move together
I melt into you

dozen red roses
velvet petals open to
a sweet smell of love

intoxication
he chose instead of my heart
love's glass is empty

子

my children walk on
paths that are different from mine
might they cross one day?

little reminders
post-it stickies everywhere
and I still forget

犬

beagle snuggled close
husband slumbers beside me
surround-sound snoring

a long day ends
laughter & tears filled the hours
a new day glimmers

朝

soft light of morning
a scent of coffee greets me
quiet solitude

shadows of leaves danced
on my skin as Moon River
played in the distance

風

leaving the harbor
a blustery wind blows, I
tack...it fills my sails

his postcard arrived
telling me of adventures
I dreamed about once

Duty called and left
too many sacrificed lives.
Always remember.

雨

my heart beats with the
pitter patter of rain, and
memories it brings

鶴

origami cranes
bright colors folded into
wishes for peace

I see a rock and
ponder it, then pick it up.
Mindless, I stack it.

月

in the full moon's light
I make believe the glow cast
upon me is love

朝

I wake early to
a solitary morning
my thoughts untangle

like the last, long slurp
of a thick chocolate shake
beloved book's last page

犬

beagle on a scent
nose pressed to the ground until
the way home is lost

We walk winding paths
lined with many memories
good friends stroll with us

朝

morning arrives but
my eyes remain closed and I
imagine you here

火

watching the fire
flames dance in her eyes making
memories ignite.

雷

dark clouds hover, our
words crash like thunder, but
silence rings louder

HAIKU

FROM

THE
RED
KIMONO

a faraway war
angry words pelt like bullets
the battle brought home

a porcelain mask
though inside a heart beats strong
even the oak breaks

today marks one year
fog blanketed memories
hide me from the light

my house is empty
but memories will remain
echoes in my heart

A stare needs no words
You are different. Go away.
A slap needs no hand.

Thanksgiving blessings
elusive as butterflies
each one a treasure

Suddenly my heart
shivers when I catch a glimpse
of Mama's cold glare

red kimono stands
starkly against winter snow
I wrap it tightly

—JANET WEBB

JUST
FOR
FUN

Sometimes for fun, I like
to summarize a book in
seventeen syllables. A few of
those "synopsis" haiku follow.

THE WIZARD OF OZ

the yellow-brick road
path to the greatest treasure
there's no place like home

GONE WITH THE WIND

Scarlett chased lost love.
When at last she loved Rhett, he
didn't give a damn.

TO KILL A MOCKINGBIRD

mischievous Scout sought
adventure, but instead found
compassion for Boo

Jan Morrill's interest in haiku comes from her Japanese heritage. Her mother, a Buddhist Japanese American, was an internee during World War II. Her father, a Southern Baptist redhead of Irish descent, retired from the Air Force. Much of Jan's writing reflects her multicultural childhood.

Jan's debut novel, a historical fiction titled *The Red Kimono*, was released by the University of Arkansas Press in February 2013. Her award-winning short stories and essays have also been published in several *Chicken Soup for the Soul* books and other anthologies.

Jan is currently working on the sequel to *The Red Kimono*.

—

FOR MORE INFORMATION, PLEASE VISIT:

www.HaikuByHaiku.wordpress.com

www.janmorrill.com.

www.ingramcontent.com/pod-product-compliance
Lightning Source LLC
Chambersburg PA
CBHW071018040426
42443CB00007B/834